SCHAUM POPULAR SERIES

Christmas-Piano Style

Arranged by John S. Hord

ISBN 978-1-5400-3457-1

Schaum

EXCLUSIVELY DISTRIBUTED BY

HAL•LEONARD®

Visit Hal Leonard Online at
www.halleonard.com

Contact Us:
Hal Leonard
7777 West Bluemound Road
Milwaukee, WI 53213
Email: info@halleonard.com

In Europe contact:
Hal Leonard Europe Limited
42 Wigmore Street
Marylebone, London, W1U 2RN
Email: info@halleonardeurope.com

In Australia contact:
Hal Leonard Australia Pty. Ltd.
4 Lentara Court
Cheltenham, Victoria, 3192 Australia
Email: info@halleonard.com.au

Contents

Deck the Hall

Traditional Welsh Carol
Arranged by John S. Hord

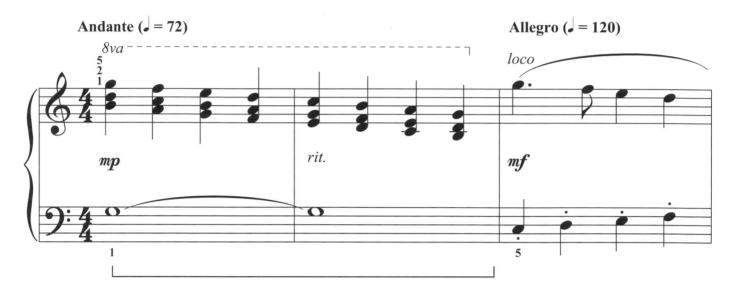

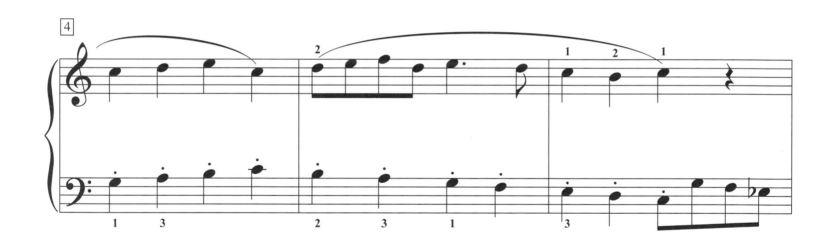

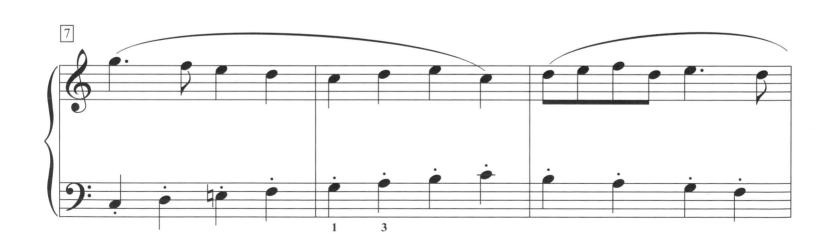

The First Noel

17th Century English Carol
Music from W. Sandys' *Christmas Carols*
Arranged by John S. Hord

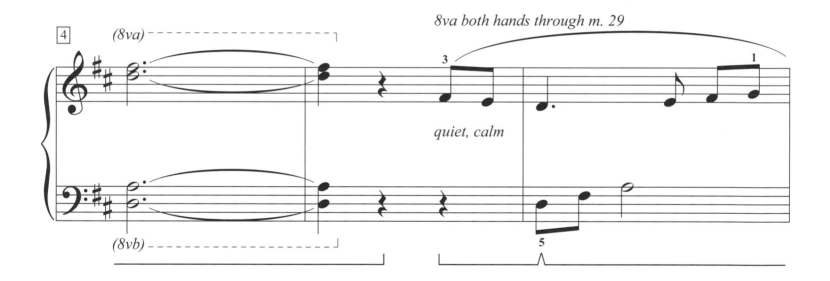

Jingle Bells

Words and Music by
J. Pierpont
Arranged by John S. Hord

Calm, smooth (♩ = 86)

God Rest Ye Merry, Gentlemen

Traditional English Carol
Arranged by John S. Hord

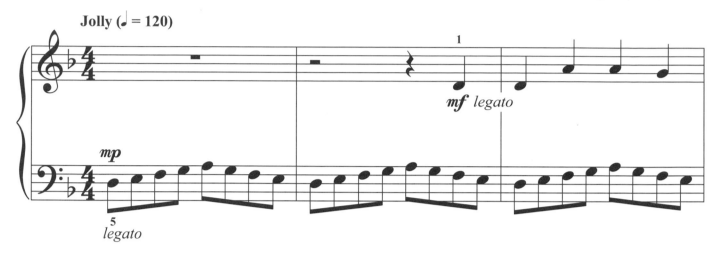

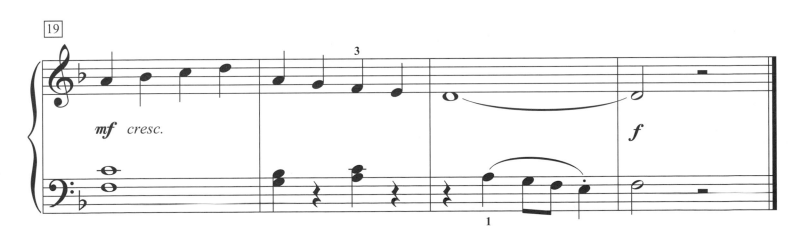

In the Bleak Midwinter

Poem by Christina Rossetti
Music by Gustav Holst
Arranged by John S. Hord

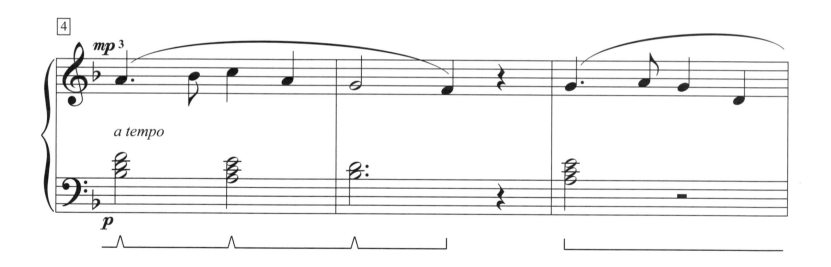

O Come, O Come Immanuel

Plainsong, 13th Century
Words translated by John M. Neale
and Henry S. Coffin
Arranged by John S. Hord

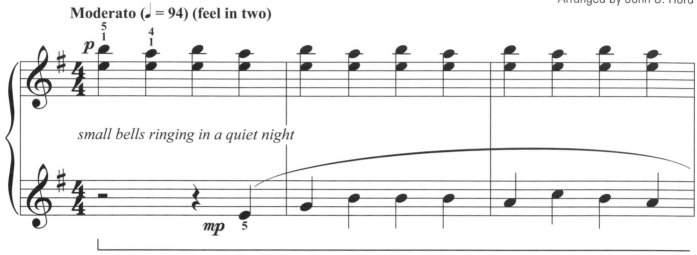

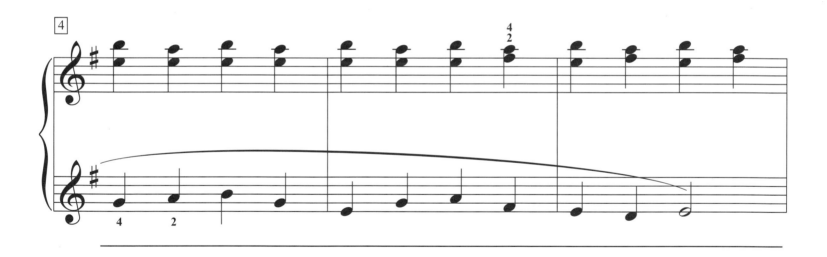

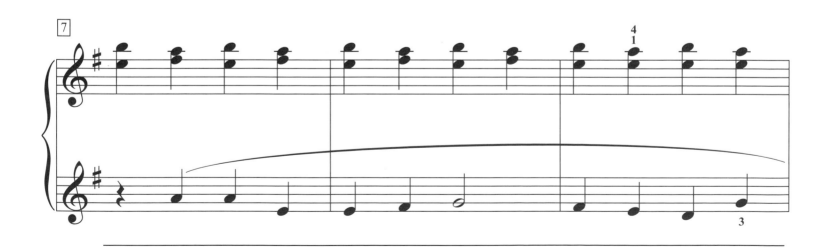

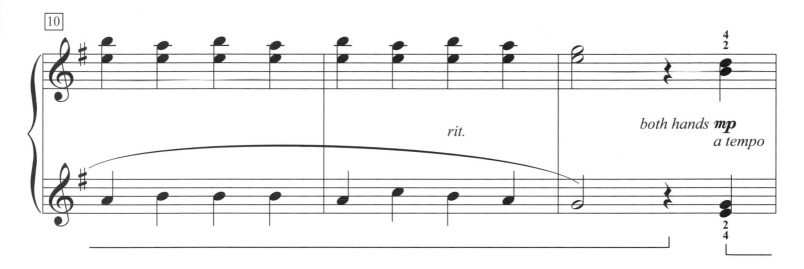

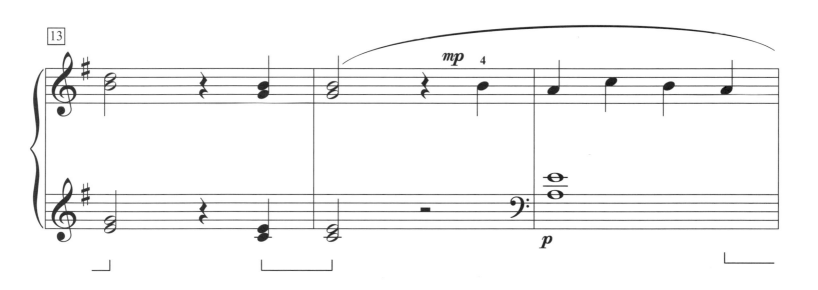

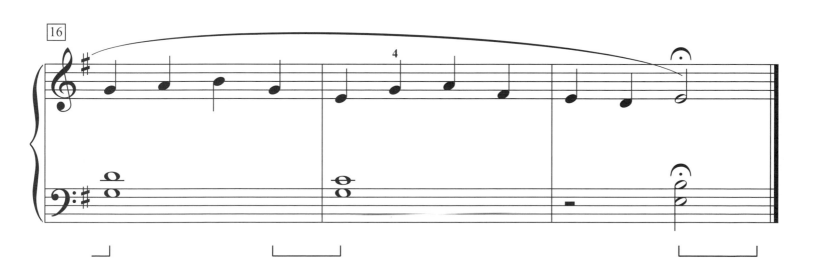

Silent Night

Words by Joseph Mohr
Translated by John F. Young
Music by Franz X. Gruber
Arranged by John S. Hord

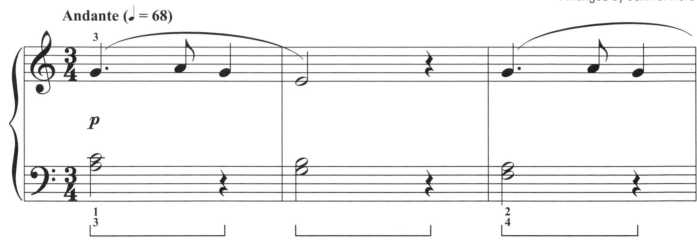

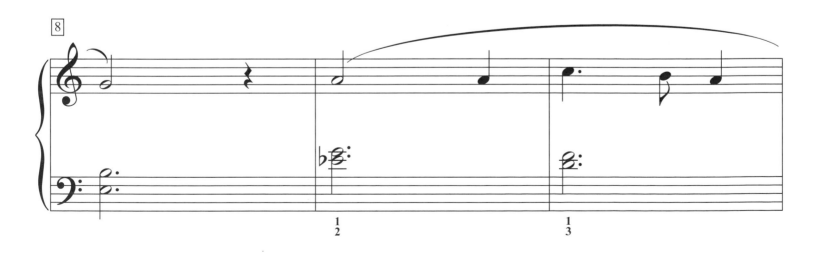

We Three Kings of Orient Are

Words and Music by
John H. Hopkins, Jr.
Arranged by John S. Hord

MORE GREAT SCHAUM PUBLICATIONS

FINGERPOWER®

by John W. Schaum

Physical training and discipline are needed for both athletics and keyboard playing. Keyboard muscle conditioning is called technic. Technic exercises are as important to the keyboard player as workouts and calisthenics are to the athlete. Schaum's *Fingerpower®* books are dedicated to development of individual finger strength and dexterity in both hands.

00645334	Primer Level – Book Only	$6.99
00645016	Primer Level – Book/Audio	$7.99
00645335	Level 1 – Book Only	$6.99
00645019	Level 1 – Book/Audio	$7.99
00645336	Level 2 – Book Only	$6.99
00645022	Level 2 – Book/Audio	$7.99
00645337	Level 3 – Book Only	$6.95
00645025	Level 3 – Book/Audio	$7.99
00645338	Level 4 – Book Only	$6.99
00645028	Level 4 – Book/Audio	$7.99
00645339	Level 5 Book Only	$6.99
00645340	Level 6 Book Only	$6.99

FINGERPOWER® ETUDES

Melodic exercises crafted by master technic composers. Modified or transposed etudes provide equal hand development with a planned variety of technical styles, key, and time signatures.

00645392	Primer Level	$6.95
00645393	Level 1	$6.99
00645394	Level 2	$6.95
00645395	Level 3	$6.95
00645396	Level 4	$6.99

FINGERPOWER® FUN

arr. Wesley Schaum
Early Elementary Level

Musical experiences beyond the traditional *Fingerpower®* books that include fun to play pieces with finger exercises and duet accompaniments. Short technic prepartory drills (finger workouts) focus on melodic patterns found in each piece.

00645126	Primer Level	$6.95
00645127	Level 1	$6.95
00645128	Level 2	$6.95
00645129	Level 3	$6.95
00645144	Level 4	$6.95

FINGERPOWER POP

Arranged by James Poteat

10 great pop piano solo arrangements with fun technical warm-ups that complement the Fingerpower series! Can also be used as motivating supplements to any method and in any learning situation.

| 00237510 | Level 1 | $9.99 |
| 00237508 | Level 2 | $9.99 |

FINGERPOWER® TRANSPOSER

by Wesley Schaum
Early Elementary Level

This book includes 21 short, 8-measure exercises using 5-finger patterns. Positions are based on C,F, and G major and no key signatures are used. Patterns involve intervals of 3rds, 4ths, and 5ths up and down and are transposed from C to F and F to C, C to G and G to C, G to F and F to G.

00645150	Primer Level	$6.95
00645151	Level 1	$6.95
00645152	Level 2	$6.95
00645154	Level 3	$6.95
00645156	Level 4	$6.95

JUMBO STAFF MANUSCRIPT BOOK

This pad features 24 pages with 4 staves per page.

00645936 . . . . $4.25

CERTIFICATE OF MUSICAL ACHIEVEMENT

Reward your students for their hard work with these official 8x10 inch certificates that you can customize. 12 per package.

00645938 . . . . $6.99

SCHAUM LESSON ASSIGNMENT BOOK

by John Schaum

With space for 32 weeks, this book will help keep students on the right track for their practice time.

00645935 . . . . $3.95

www.halleonard.com

Prices, contents, and availability subject to change without notice.

Big Fun with Big-Note Piano Books!

These songbooks feature exciting easy arrangements for beginning piano students.

Best of Adele
Now even beginners can play their favorite Adele tunes! This book features big-note arrangements of 10 top songs: Chasing Pavements • Daydreamer • Hometown Glory • Lovesong • Make You Feel My Love • One and Only • Rolling in the Deep • Set Fire to the Rain • Someone like You • Turning Tables.
00308601 .... $12.99

Beatles' Best
27 classics for beginners to enjoy, including: Can't Buy Me Love • Eleanor Rigby • Hey Jude • Michelle • Here, There and Everywhere • When I'm Sixty-Four • Yesterday • and more.
00222561 .... $14.99

The Best Songs Ever
70 favorites, featuring: Body and Soul • Crazy • Edelweiss • Fly Me to the Moon • Georgia on My Mind • Imagine • The Lady Is a Tramp • Memory • A String of Pearls • Tears in Heaven • Unforgettable • You Are So Beautiful • and more.
00310425 .... $19.95

Children's Favorite Movie Songs
arranged by Phillip Keveren
16 favorites from films, including: The Bare Necessities • Beauty and the Beast • Can You Feel the Love Tonight • Do-Re-Mi • The Rainbow Connection • Tomorrow • Zip-A-Dee-Doo-Dah • and more.
00310838 .... $12.99

Classical Music's Greatest Hits
24 beloved classical pieces, including: Air on the G String • Ave Maria • By the Beautiful Blue Danube • Canon in D • Eine Kleine Nachtmusik • Für Elise • Ode to Joy • Romeo and Juliet • Waltz of the Flowers • more.
00310475 .... $12.99

Disney Big-Note Collection
Over 40 Disney favorites, including: Circle of Life • Colors of the Wind • Hakuna Matata • It's a Small World • Under the Sea • A Whole New World • Winnie the Pooh • Zip-A-Dee-Doo-Dah • and more.
00316056 .... $19.99

Essential Classical
22 simplified piano pieces from top composers, including: Ave Maria (Schubert) • Blue Danube Waltz (Strauss) • Für Elise (Beethoven) • Jesu, Joy of Man's Desiring (Bach) • Morning (Grieg) • Pomp and Circumstance (Elgar) • and many more.
00311205 .... $10.99

Favorite Children's Songs
arranged by Bill Boyd
29 easy arrangements of songs to play and sing with children: Peter Cottontail • I Whistle a Happy Tune • It's a Small World • On the Good Ship Lollipop • The Rainbow Connection • and more!
00240251 .... $12.99

Frozen
9 songs from this hit Disney film, plus full-color illustrations from the movie. Songs include the standout single "Let It Go," plus: Do You Want to Build a Snowman? • For the First Time in Forever • Reindeer(s) Are Better Than People • and more.
00126105 .... $12.99

Happy Birthday to You and Other Great Songs for Big-Note Piano
16 essential favorites, including: Chitty Chitty Bang Bang • Good Night • Happy Birthday to You • Heart and Soul • Over the Rainbow • Sing • This Land Is Your Land • and more.
00119636 .... $9.99

Elton John – Greatest Hits
20 of his biggest hits, including: Bennie and the Jets • Candle in the Wind • Crocodile Rock • Rocket Man • Tiny Dancer • Your Song • and more.
00221832 .... $12.99

Les Misérables
14 favorites from the Broadway sensation arranged for beginning pianists. Titles include: At the End of the Day • Bring Him Home • Castle on a Cloud • I Dreamed a Dream • In My Life • On My Own • Who Am I? • and more.
00221812 .... $15.99

The Phantom of the Opera
9 songs from the Broadway spectacular, including: All I Ask of You • Angel of Music • Masquerade • The Music of the Night • The Phantom of the Opera • The Point of No Return • Prima Donna • Think of Me • Wishing You Were Somehow Here Again.
00110006 .... $14.99

Pride & Prejudice
Music from the Motion Picture Soundtrack
12 piano pieces from the 2006 Oscar-nominated film: Another Dance • Darcy's Letter • Georgiana • Leaving Netherfield • Liz on Top of the World • Meryton Townhall • The Secret Life of Daydreams • Stars and Butterflies • and more.
00316125 .... $12.99

The Sound of Music
arranged by Phillip Keveren
9 favorites: Climb Ev'ry Mountain • Do-Re-Mi • Edelweiss • The Lonely Goatherd • Maria • My Favorite Things • Sixteen Going on Seventeen • So Long, Farewell • The Sound of Music.
00316057 .... $10.99

Best of Taylor Swift
A dozen top tunes from this crossover sensation: Fearless • Fifteen • Hey Stephen • Love Story • Our Song • Picture to Burn • Teardrops on My Guitar • White Horse • You Belong with Me • and more.
00307143 .... $12.99

Worship Favorites
20 powerful songs: Above All • Come, Now Is the Time to Worship • I Could Sing of Your Love Forever • More Precious Than Silver • Open the Eyes of My Heart • Shout to the Lord • and more.
00311207 .... $12.99

Complete song lists online at
www.halleonard.com

0818
060